Little Tiger Hu can Roar!

T0384540

by Gabby Pritchard
illustrated by Galia Bernstein

CAMBRIDGE
UNIVERSITY PRESS

Institute of Education

Little Tiger Hu was very happy.

'I can ROAR,' he said.

It was a BIG and SCARY roar!

'I can play a game,' he said.

Tiger Hu saw Elephant.

Slowly, slowly he went through the long grass.

'One, two, three, four . . . '

'**HELP**!' shouted Elephant and he ran into the forest.

Little Tiger Hu saw Hippo.
Slowly, slowly he went round
the big rocks.

'One, two, three, four . . .'

'**HELP**!' shouted Hippo and he jumped
into the river.

Little Tiger Hu saw Monkey.

Slowly, slowly he climbed up a tree.

'One, two, three, four . . . '

'**HELP**!' shouted Monkey and he ran
up a big tree.

Little Tiger Hu saw Hare.

Slowly, slowly he went over a bridge . . .

. . . into a green field.

'One, two, three, four . . .'

'Hello, Little Tiger Hu,' said Hare.

'Why aren't you scared?' said Little Tiger Hu.

'You are silly,' said Hare. 'Babies are not scary, even if they have a big roar.'

'We can play a new game,'
said Little Tiger Hu.

Little Tiger Hu and Hare went to play
in the forest.

Little Tiger Hu can Roar!   Gabby Pritchard

Teaching notes written by Sue Bodman and Glen Franklin

Using this book

Developing reading comprehension

This humorous story follows a pattern seen in many traditional tales where a sequence is built up over several episodes. Little Tiger Hu has recently learned how to roar. He creeps up behind several animals as they are feeding – Elephant, Hippo and Monkey – enjoying scaring them, only to find that Hare is not scared.

This text has some simple literary language which may need to be supported. At Yellow band, the reader has to make some deductions about the characters in the story to get the full meaning. Here, Little Tiger Hu is a baby trying out a new skill and that inference is an important element in understanding why Hare is not scared.

Grammar and sentence structure

- The position of the adverb at the beginning of the sentence for dramatic effect - '*Slowly, slowly he went ...*'
- Complex sentence - '*even if they have a big roar.*' (page 12)

Word meaning and spelling

- Check knowledge of prepositions *over, into, through.*
- Reinforce 'ee' words in context *three, tree, see, green.*

Curriculum links

Geography – Little Tiger Hu creeps up on the animals by moving around the forest and the field. This context could be used to develop geography activities, mapping landscape features and creating routes around different landscapes.

Music – Listening activities using different environmental sounds could build on the idea of listening carefully to the sounds around you.

Learning Outcomes

Children can:

- read more challenging texts using phonic knowledge along with automatic recognition of high-frequency words
- use syntax and context when reading for meaning
- interpret a text by reading aloud with some variety of pace and emphasis
- comment on events, characters, and ideas, making imaginative links to their own experience.

A guided reading lesson

Introducing the text

Give a book to each child and read the title.

Orientation

Give a brief orientation to the text: *In this story, Little Tiger Hu likes playing games. He makes other animals in the jungle jump. How do you think he does that?*

Preparation

Pages 2 and 3: Here we can see Little Tiger Hu practising his roar. He creeps up on Elephant. Find where it says 'Slowly, slowly, he went through the long grass'. Practise saying that to yourself. Elephant doesn't see him. What do you think will happen next?

Page 4. Were you right? Who does Litte Tiger Hu creep up on next?

He makes more animals jump until

Pages 10 and 11: Do you think that Hare is scared? Why?/Why not?

Let's read the story and find out.